SOMEONE TO LISTEN

Everybody is busy, busy, busy. They have no time to stop and listen to each other. With some hard work and patience, the children create a meal that their whole community can enjoy, finding friendship along the way.

With growing concerns around mental health, and in the wake of a period of uncertainty and change, it is more important than ever to pay attention to how young children express their emotions, and to teach them to articulate their thoughts in a healthy way. This beautifully illustrated picture book has been created to help children understand the importance of having someone to listen to you. Children are encouraged to think about how characters might be feeling at different points in the story and think about what makes the characters feel valued.

When it comes to child and adolescent mental health issues, prevention and early intervention are key. The 'serve and return' format of this book provides a virtual space where children can explore thoughts and feelings, teaching them that they have a place in their community.

Louise Jackson is a teacher, trainer and author who draws on her direct experience of working with children in schools to develop educational materials that are designed to promote participation, relationships and conversation. She has worked on 'closing the gap' projects with national charities, local authorities, schools, children's centres and training organisations to address educational disadvantage, finding new ways to build capacity and resilience across early childhood services and local communities.

Privileged to have worked alongside many inspirational teachers, practitioners and volunteers in educational settings where vulnerable children are thriving, Louise seeks to capture in her research and writing what it is that makes the difference for young children. Working in collaboration with illustrator Katie Waller, she has created a series of books and practical tools which will help local communities, parents, practitioners and teachers understand the valuable role they can all play in cultivating resilience in early childhood.

A practical guide for early years practitioners
and four children's picture books to
use with 4–6-year-olds.

SOMEONE TO LISTEN

A Thought Bubbles Picture Book About Finding Friends

Louise Jackson
Illustrated by Katie Waller

Routledge
Taylor & Francis Group

LONDON AND NEW YORK

Cover image credit: Katie Waller

First published 2022
by Routledge
2 Park Square, Milton Park, Abingdon, Oxon OX14 4RN

and by Routledge
605 Third Avenue, New York, NY 10158

Routledge is an imprint of the Taylor & Francis Group, an informa business

British Library Cataloguing-in-Publication Data
A catalogue record for this book is available from the British Library

Library of Congress Cataloging-in-Publication Data
Names: Jackson, Louise, 1964- author. | Waller, Katie, illustrator.
Title: Someone to listen : a thought bubbles picture book about finding friends / Louise Jackson ; illustrated by Katie Waller.
Description: Milton Park, Abingdon, Oxon ; New York, NY : Routledge, 2022.
Identifiers: LCCN 2021028607 (print) | LCCN 2021028608 (ebook) | ISBN 9781032135892 (paperback) | ISBN 9781003230007 (ebook)
Subjects: LCSH: Friendship in children--Juvenile literature. | Emotions in children--Juvenile literature. | Interpersonal communication in children--Juvenile literature.
Classification: LCC BF723.F68 J33 2022 (print) | LCC BF723.F68 (ebook) | DDC 155.4/1925--dc23/eng/20211006
LC record available at https://lccn.loc.gov/2021028607
LC ebook record available at https://lccn.loc.gov/2021028608

ISBN: 978-1-032-13589-2 (pbk)
ISBN: 978-1-003-23000-7 (ebk)

DOI: 10.4324/9781003230007

Typeset in Madeleina Sans
by Deanta Global Publishing Services, Chennai, India

The crowd
hustled and bustled,
moving this way
and that.

So much to do,
it's crazy!

So little
time to spare!

Get out – Move Away!

YOU CAN'T STAND THERE!

There's nothing you can do.

Be off with you now.

Just GO!

Out of the earth,
the dust and the scrub,
the smallest shoot
began
to
grow ...

... And grow

... And GROW

... AND GROW!

The children watched ... The children waited.

The children watered ... and they waited.

Time went slowly as the bumble bees buzzed.

Birds sang out whilst butterflies fluttered by ... and by ... and by.

Here in the garden new friendships began.

Talking together, a helping hand.

Pumpkins, carrots, runner beans and redcurrants.

Radishes, beetroot, broccoli and marrow.

A picnic lunch ... we've got lots to share.

Come on in ...

everyone is here!

'Hey! What's this?' – the people said.

'Something new, a garden shed?
We didn't know, we didn't help,
it's looking good' – the people said.

Here in the garden,
new friendships began.
Everyone with time to listen,
everyone with time to care.

A picnic lunch on a garden bench.